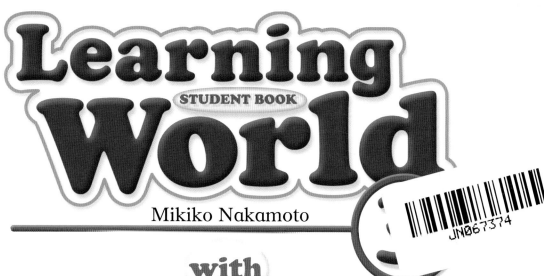

Learning World
STUDENT BOOK

Mikiko Nakamoto

JN067374

with

Jim

Sally

Jason

Tina

Mary

Let's communicate in English!

grandmother

Zippy

Sakura

grandfather

Mr. Kobayashi

Shota

Mrs. Kobayashi

ラーニングワールドシリーズは9巻から成り、幼児〜小学高学年までそれぞれの発達段階に応じて書かれています。本シリーズはヒューマニスティック・アプローチとコミュニカティブ・アプローチを取り入れ、従来の、暗記とパターンプラクティス中心の英語教育ではなく、「答えが1つでない」英語による言語教育を目指しています。子供達の発話に重要な「自分の意見の構築」「自尊心の育成」「他社への許容」等が英語の四技能の学習を通して習得できるようにしています。また、子供達の日常生活に合ったチャンツ、会話、歌などで目標文が無理なく効果的に定着できます。テキストは10ユニットあり、各レッスンにインフォメーションギャップのあるコミュニケーション活動を紹介しています。本テキストでは年度末の1か月をかけて「総復習と到達度評価のためのAchievement Targets (p.3)」の17の課題を達成することを目指します。2024年発刊の 3rd Edition では音声とチャンツ動画のQRコードを付し、各右ページで使う語彙や英文の音声を追加しました。

● **このテキストには、次のマークが入っています。なにをするのか、見てわかるようになりましょう。** ●

Words
単語をおぼえましょう。

Communication activity
英語を使って、友達や先生と協力して、活動しましょう。

Dialog
会話文をおぼえましょう。

Let's Make a Speech
自分の考えを、みんなの前で発表しましょう。

Chant
リズムにのっておぼえましょう。

Drill
問題を解きましょう。

Speech
スピーチをおぼえましょう。

Song
歌いましょう。

Story
ストーリーの内容をおぼえましょう。

Phonics
読んでみましょう。

Letter
手紙の内容をおぼえましょう。

Listening Test
英語を聞いて答えましょう。
どれだけ聞きとれるかな？

● 家で音声を聞きましょう。 **3→4**　　　● チャンツ動画を楽しく活用しましょう。

A to Z

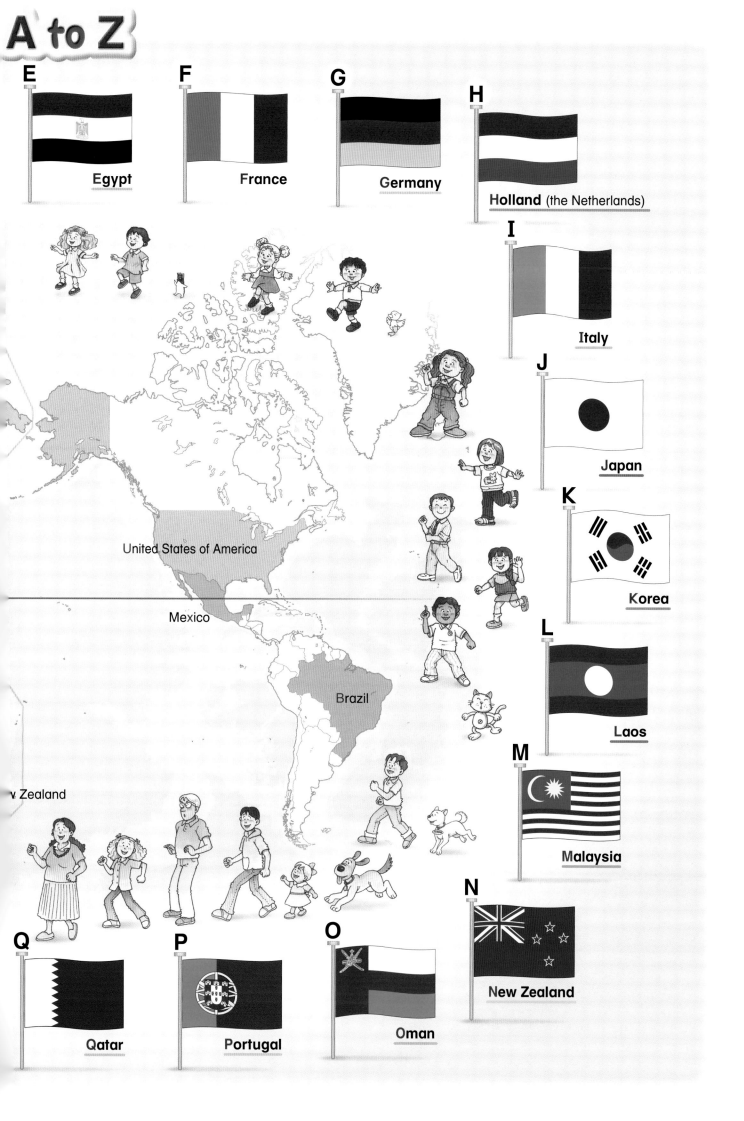

E Egypt

F France

G Germany

H **Holland** (the Netherlands)

I **Italy**

J **Japan**

K **Korea**

L **Laos**

M **Malaysia**

N **New Zealand**

United States of America

Mexico

Brazil

v Zealand

Q **Qatar**

P **Portugal**

O **Oman**

CONTENTS

これだけできるようにがんばろう。

1 自分の通っている学校と学年を言うことができます。
Able to say the school I go to and what grade I am in.

2 人物を1人選び、8つ以上の文を使って紹介することができます。
Able to introduce a person using more than 8 sentences.

3 先生に「〜しなさい」「〜してはいけません」という命令が4つできます。
Able to give four "Do this." or "Don't do this." orders to my teacher.

4 There is…, There are… を使って教室内にあるものを5つ言うことができます。
Able to say five things in the classroom using "There is a … There are …s".

5 I want to go to… を使って行きたい国を言うことができます。
Able to say what country I want to go to.

6 昨日したことを5つ言うことができます。
Able to say what I did yesterday.

7 昨夜の9時にしていたことを言うことができます。
Able to say what I was doing at nine o'clock last night.

8 2つのものを選んで比べる文を言うことができます。
Able to say two things using comparative form.

9 先生や友達に10個の質問をし、その答えをみんなに伝えることができます。
Able to ask 10 questions to my teacher/friends and tell everyone the answers.
○○○○○○○○○○ (If you can say it, color ○)

10 テキストの中のチャンツ ⬤ を8つ、暗唱できます。
Able to recite eight chants
from the CHANTS pages. ⑩ ⑫ ⑭ ⑯ ㉒ ㉚ ㉞ ㊱ ㊻ ㊽ ㊾ 52 54

11 テキストの中のダイアログ ⬤ を5つ、友達と一緒に暗記で言えます。
Able to say five dialogs
from the DIALOG pages with my friend. ⑥ ⑳ ㉖ ㉜ ㊵ ㊷ ㊹

12 テキストの中の歌 ♪ を3曲歌うことができます。
Able to sing three songs from the SONG pages. ⑤ ⑮ ⑰ ⑲ ㉓ 53

13 テキストの中の文 ⬤ を5つ暗唱することができます。
Able to recite five speeches from the SPEECH pages. ④ ⑧ ⑱ ㉔ ㉘ ㊳ 50 58 60

14 テキストの中のストーリー ⬤ を1つ暗唱することができます。
Able to recite one story from the STORY pages in a loud voice. 56 62

15 先生が見せるカードを20個正しく読むことができます。
Able to read twenty words/expressions my teacher shows me correctly.

16 テキストの左ページの英語をノートに全ページ書き写しました。
Copied all the pages of English on the left page of the text into my notebook.

17 自分のことを10以上の文を使ってはっきり言うことができます。
Able to give a speech about myself clearly using in 10 or more sentences.

○の中の数字はページをあらわしています。

I love the sun.

I love the trees.

I love the moon.

I love the sky.

And I love you best of all.

5

Words

sun   tree   moon   sky   mountain   hill   flower   lake   cloud   star

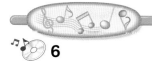

- Whose information is this?
- It is Ms. Matsunaga's information.

■))**150**

♪ 6

I Love the Mountains

(Bundi ada, Bundi ada, Bundi ada, Bundi ada.
Bundi ada, Bundi ada, Bundi ada, Bundi ada.)
I love the mountains, I love the rolling hills,
I love the flowers, I love the daffodils,
I love the fireside, when all the lights are low. (×2)

( ) repeat

daffodil

fireside

rolling hills

Let's Make a Speech

I love

_____,

I love

_____.

And I love

_____ best of all.

7→8

Hello. My name is Tina.

My family name is Barton.

Hello. My name is Shota.

My family name is Kobayashi.

We go to Lakeside Elementary School.

We are in the fifth grade.

We live in Denver, Colorado, in the U.S.

It is a beautiful city.

We love our city.

9

Words

| in the ... grade | first | second | third | fourth | fifth | sixth |

2B

Communication activity

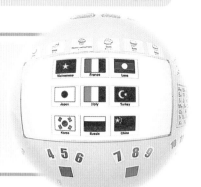

○ I live in Japan.

○ I love my country.

🔊151

Hello, everyone. I'm happy to be here.

My name is _____ .

My family name is _____ .

I'm _____ years old.

I'm glad to meet you all. Thank you.

1
- (a) sunny
- (b) rainy
- (c) cloudy
- (d) two o'clock

2
- (a) April 14th
- (b) May 14th
- (c) sunny
- (d) mother

3
- (a) mother
- (b) father
- (c) a dog
- (d) a cat

4
- (a) Sunday
- (b) Friday
- (c) April 14th
- (d) June 14th

5
- (a) January
- (b) Sunday
- (c) two o'clock
- (d) April 14th

6
- (a) two o'clock
- (b) sunny
- (c) April 14th
- (d) mother

 Let me introduce my family.

The Bartons

This is my mother. Her name is Sally.
She is a firefighter.

This is my father. His name is Jim.
He is a taxi driver.

This is my big brother. His name is Jason.
He is a student.

This is my little sister. Her name is Mary.

This is my dog. His name is Zippy.

12

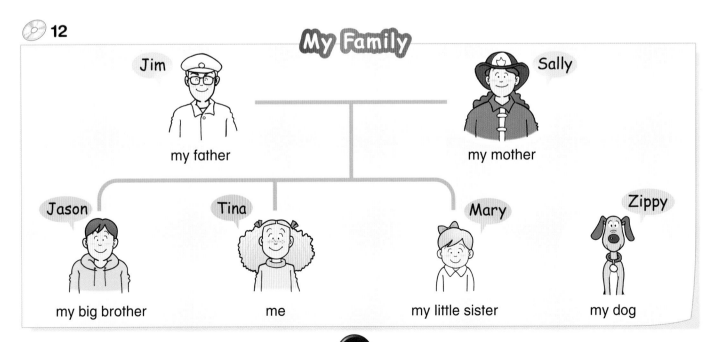

My Family

Jim — my father

Sally — my mother

Jason — my big brother

Tina — me

Mary — my little sister

Zippy — my dog

3B

Communication activity

🔊152

● Where do you live?
● What do you do?
● What do you want?

Survival English

 🔊101

①	職員室や教室に入る時は	May I come in?
②	先生と別れる時は	Goodbye. See you tomorrow. / See you next week.
③	答えを知らない時は	I don't know.
④	答えをわすれた時は	I forgot. / I forget.
⑤	質問の意味がわからない時は	I don't understand.
⑥	少し待ってほしい時は	Just a moment, please.
⑦	よく聞こえなかった時は	Once more, please.
⑧	もっとゆっくり話してほしい時は	More slowly, please.
⑨	考えている時は	I'm thinking.
⑩	英語で何と言うかわからない時は	How do you say … in English?
⑪	遅刻したら	I'm sorry I'm late.
⑫	作業ができたら	I'm finished!
⑬	友達に消しゴムを借りる時は	May I use your eraser?
⑭	単語の読み方を聞く時は	How do you say this word?
⑮	単語の書き方を聞く時は	How do you spell …?

13 → 14

What does he do? What does he do?

He is brave and he is strong.

A police officer? — No.

A dentist? — No.

A teacher? — No.

A taxi driver?

Yes. A brave, strong taxi driver.

What does she do? What does she do?

She is brave and she is strong.

A doctor? — No.

A nurse? — No.

A scientist? — No.

A firefighter?

Yes. A brave, strong firefighter.

15

Words

firefighter   taxi driver   police officer   engineer   carpenter   farmer   fisherman

1B

Communication activity

◉ Is he a firefighter?

◉ Yes, he is. / No, he isn't.

🔊 153

I am thirty years old.

Hello. My name is _____ .

I am _____ .

I live in _____ .

I have _____ .

I like _____ .

I don't like _____ .

I want _____ .

I can _____ .

16→17

Busy, busy, busy.
We are busy all day long.

Mom is cooking all day long.

Dad is shopping all day long.

I am washing all day long.

Jason is cleaning all day long.

Mary is crying all day long.

Zippy is running all day long.

Busy, busy, busy.
We are busy all day long.

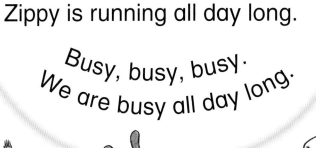

note

is	
am	~ing
are	

running

18 **Words**

 cooking   shopping   washing   cleaning    crying

 practicing the piano   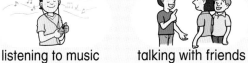 driving a car   listening to music   talking with friends   waiting for a bus

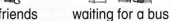

Communication activity

🔊154

○ What is Mother doing?

○ She is cooking.

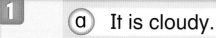
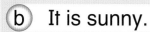

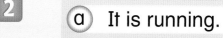

1		2	
ⓐ It is cloudy.		ⓐ It is running.	
ⓑ It is sunny.		ⓑ It is sleeping.	
ⓒ It is ten o'clock.		ⓒ It is cooking.	

3		4	
ⓐ It is Sunday.		ⓐ Three.	
ⓑ It is ten o'clock.		ⓑ Four.	
ⓒ It is May third.		ⓒ One.	

19 → 20

Do this. Do that.   Don't do that.
Do this. Do that.   Don't do that.

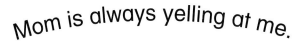

Mom is always yelling at me.

Do your homework.   Don't go out.
Make your bed.   Don't jump around.
Eat more slowly.   Don't make noise.
Go to bed.   Don't stay up late.
Behave yourself.   Be a good boy.
  Do this. Do that.   Don't do that.
  Do this. Do that.   Don't do that.

Can't you hear her yelling at me?

note

Go out.   Don't go out.

21 **Words**

make your bed   stay up late   jump around   make noise   eat more slowly

be a good boy
behave yourself
yell at me

Communication activity

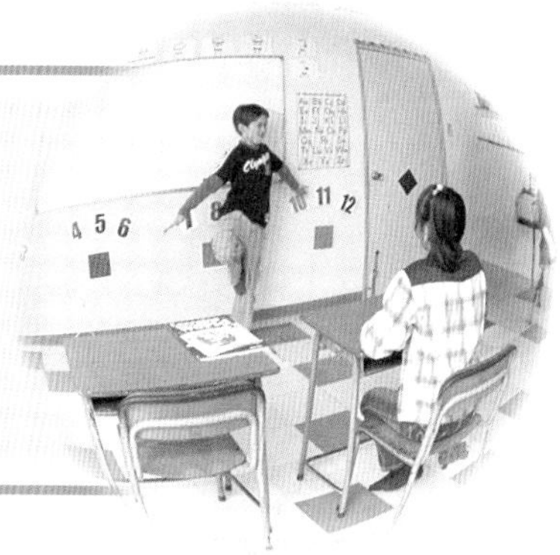

🔊155

- Do this. Do that.
- Don't do that.

22

Did you ever see a lassie?

① Did you ever see a lassie, a lassie, a lassie?
Did you ever see a lassie, go this way and that?
Go this way and that way, and this way and that way,
Did you ever see a lassie, go this way and that?

② Did you ever see a laddie, a laddie, a laddie?
Did you ever see a laddie, go this way and that?
Go this way and that way, and this way and that way,
Did you ever see a laddie, go this way and that?

Start

lip rip

read lead read lead

ring ling ring ling ring

right light right light right light

race lace race lace race lace race

lock rock lock rock lock rock lock rock

wrong long wrong long wrong long wrong long wrong

1 2 3 4 5 6 7 8 9

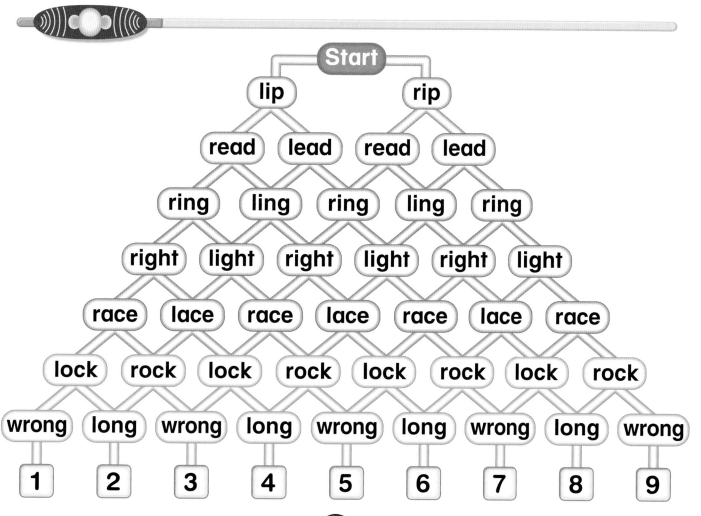

Unit **3** *1A*

23→24

A dog.　　Look!　More than one.　DOGS!

A cat.　　Look!　More than one.　CATS!

A pig.　　Look!　More than one.　PIGS!

A goose.　Look!　More than one.　GEESE!

A mouse.　Look!　More than one.　MICE!

A sheep.　Look!　More than one.　Well… SHEEP!

25

words

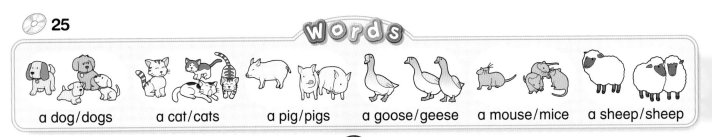

a dog/dogs　　a cat/cats　　a pig/pigs　　a goose/geese　　a mouse/mice　　a sheep/sheep

1B

Communication activity

🔊**156**

○ **How many mice?**

○ **Three mice.**

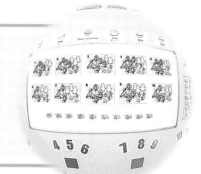

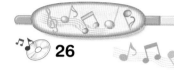

🎵💿 **26**

One Man Went to Mow

① *One man* went to mow, went to mow a meadow.
One man and his dog went to mow a meadow.

② *Two cats* went to mow, went to mow a meadow.
Two cats, one man, and his dog
went to mow a meadow.

③ *Three pigs* went to mow, went to mow a meadow.
Three pigs, two cats, one man, and his dog
went to mow a meadow.

④ *Four geese* went to mow, went to mow a meadow.
Four geese, three pigs, two cats, one man, and his dog
went to mow a meadow.

⑤ *Five mice* went to mow, went to mow a meadow.
Five mice, four geese, three pigs, two cats, one man, and his dog
went to mow a meadow.

and one man

went to mow a meadow.

■ The picture is No.   .

There is a barn   on a farm.
There is a pig   on the barn.
There is a cow   on the pig.
There is a horse   on the cow.
There is a duck   on the horse.
There is a turkey   on the duck.
There are five chicks   on the turkey.
Watch out!

There is **a cow** on the pig.   There are **chicks** on the turkey.

barn   farm   cow   horse   duck   turkey   a chick/chicks   a child/children

29

Communication activity

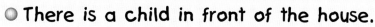

🔊 157

- There is a child in front of the house.
- There are three children between the house and the tree.
- There are two children in the house.
- There is a child on the roof.

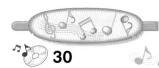 30

Old MacDonald Had a Farm

① Old MacDonald had a farm, E-I-E-I-O,
And on his farm he had some cows, E-I-E-I-O,
With a moo-moo here, and a moo-moo there,
Here a moo, there a moo, everywhere a moo-moo,
Old MacDonald had a farm, E-I-E-I-O,

② ......And on his farm he had some chicks, ...With a chick-chick here,...
③ ......And on his farm he had some ducks, ...With a quack-quack here,...
④ ......And on his farm he had some pigs, ...With an oink-oink here,...
⑤ ......And on his farm he had some turkeys, ...With a gobble-gobble here,...
⑥ ......And on his farm he had some horses, ...With a neigh-neigh here,...

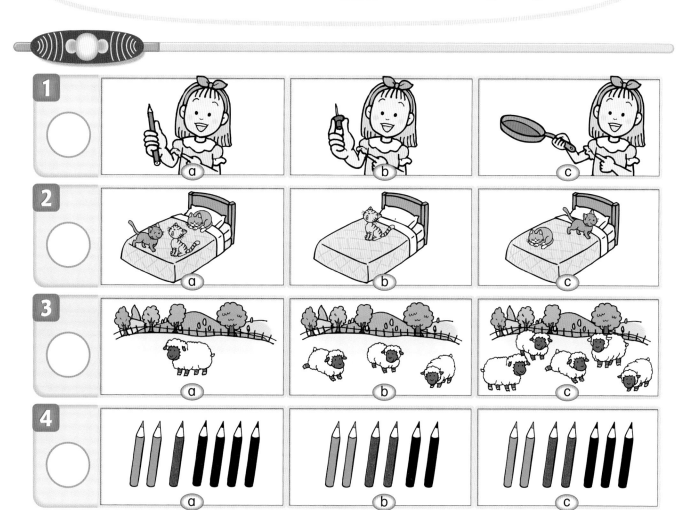

 Which car is yours?

 That big car is mine.

 Which one?

 That big purple car is mine.

 Which one?

 That big purple car between the small red car

and the big red car is mine.

 Oh, I see. That one is yours!

note

Three beautiful small shiny new yellow cars.

Communication activity

◉))158

- Which car is yours?
- That big purple car between the small red car and the big red car is mine.

yellow

pink

yellow

blue

yellow

blue

My Flower Bed

pink

12

11

5

blue

pink

pink

blue

yellow

10

9

8

7

6

I like the _____ flower

between the _____ flower

and the _____ flower.

Phonics

◉))135

c

city

cent

cat

g

giant

gym

gun

 33 → 34

 I can't swim.

 Yes, you can.

 I can't swim.

 Yes, you can.

 I can't swim.

 Yes, you can.

Try it, try it, you can do it.

 I made it, I made it, I made it. All right!

 You made it, you made it, you made it. All right!

35

Words

| dive | win | score a goal | score a basket | jump over |

| bake a cake | ride a unicycle | make a speech | I made it! | You made it! |

Communication activity

🔊159

○ **Can you dance?**

○ **Yes, I can. / No, I can't.**

What can you do?

I can

I can't

swim 100 meters	cook *sukiyaki*	eat green peppers

hold my breath for 1 minute   stand on one leg for 3 minutes

🔊102

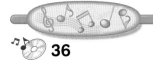

🎵 36   ***What Can You Do?***

I can walk, I can jump, and I can run.   Yes, we can!
I can see, I can hear, and I can smile.   Yes, we can!
I can learn, I can play, and I can think.
I can make you happy, and you can make me happy. (×2)

This is my friend. I am proud of my friend.

He can go everywhere in his wheelchair.

He can play basketball, too.

He is a great athlete.

This is my dog. I am proud of my dog.

I can go everywhere with him.

He can stop at the red lights.

He is a smart guide dog.

harness

39

Words

wheelchair

athlete

smart

guide dog

great

I'm proud of …
everywhere

Communication activity

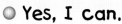

🔊160

- Can you read Braille?
- Yes, I can.
- What does it say?
- It says "cap."

This is my _____.

I am proud of my _____.

$\left(\begin{array}{c} \text{He} \\ \text{She} \end{array}\right)$ can _____.

Each Braille word is enclosed by " ⠲ ⠂.

1

hope _____ _____

2

love   world   school

1 (   )

2 (   )

3 (   )

4 (   )

 Can you speak Japanese?

 Of course I can.

I can speak Japanese very well.

I am from Japan.

Can you speak Japanese?

Yes, I can. But just a little.

I can say "*Watashi no namae wa Tina desu.*"

Can Jason speak Japanese?

He can't speak Japanese at all.

42

Words

very well

How are you?

I am glad to meet you.

Hi!

I'm ...

I can speak English **very well**.

a little

How are you?
I... I...
I am ...

I can speak English **a little**.

not ... at all

I cannot speak English **at all**.

Communication activity

● Can you speak French?

● Yes, I can. I can speak French very well.

◀))161

Can you … ?

	very well	well	a little	not … at all
① swim				
② play the piano				
③ play the recorder				
④ ski				
⑤ cook				
⑥ speak French				
⑦ speak English				
⑧ write English				

◀))136

 ee

see

bee

meet

 ea

sea

tea

meat

 Shota is my best friend.

He is from Kobe, Japan.

Shota has a dog, Sakura.

Sakura means cherry blossoms in Japanese.

His father, Mr. Kobayashi, is an engineer.

He is building a big bridge.

His mother, Mrs. Kobayashi, goes to college.

She is studying English.

Shota speaks English and Japanese.

note

I
have

he
has   she
has

you
have

45

Words

live→lives   have→has   like→likes   go→goes   speak→speaks   eat→eats   mean→means

Communication activity

- What is it?

- It has six legs.
- It likes sugar.

))162

What is it?

① It can't fly.
It has four legs.
It is strong.
It is big.
It has a long nose.
What is it?

It is an _____ .

② It is small.
It can jump.
It likes carrots.
It has long ears.
It has red eyes.
What is it?

It is a _____ .

lion

snake

kangaroo

rabbit

dinosaur

elephant

monkey

fox

giraffe

③ It can't swim.
It can run fast.
It is tall.
It has a long neck.
What is it?

It is a _____ .

④ It can swim.
It can move fast.
It is long.
It doesn't have legs.
What is it?

It is a _____ .

Who is it?

It is a cat.

It can fly.
It doesn't have ears.
It doesn't like mice.
It is a robot.
It has a big pocket.
It likes *dorayaki.*

46→47

Do you like me? **No, we don't.**

Yes, you do. No, we don't.

Yes, you do. No, we don't.

Yes, you do. All right, we like you.

Does he like me? **No, he doesn't.**

Yes, he does. No, he doesn't.

Yes, he does. No, he doesn't.

Yes, he does. All right, he likes you.

Does she like me? **No, she doesn't.**

Yes, she does. No, she doesn't.

Yes, she does. No, she doesn't.

Yes, she does. All right, she likes you.

note

Do you like me?	Yes, I do.	Does she like me?	Yes, she does.
	No, I don't.		No, she doesn't.

2B Unit 5

Communication activity

◯ Does she live in Kyoto?

◯ Yes, she does. / No, she doesn't.

🔊)163

① (He, She) is a (boy, girl).

② (He, She) lives in ….

③ (He, She) (likes, doesn't like)….

④ (He, She) (has, doesn't have)….

⑤ (He, She)….

1 (   )

2 (   )

3 (   )

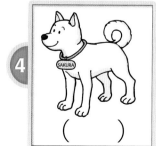

4 (   )

31
thirty-one

48→49

 Who cleans your room?

 I do.

 Who cooks breakfast?

 My mother does.

 Who washes the dishes?

 My father does.

 Who feeds Zippy?

 Mary does.

 What does Jason do?

 He doesn't do anything!

note

Who cleans your room?

I do.

My father does.

50

words

clean (your) room   cook breakfast   wash the dishes

buy groceries   clean the bathroom   feed the pet

Communication activity

- Who cleans your room?
- Tina does. Mother does, too.

📢 **164**

Who does what in your family?

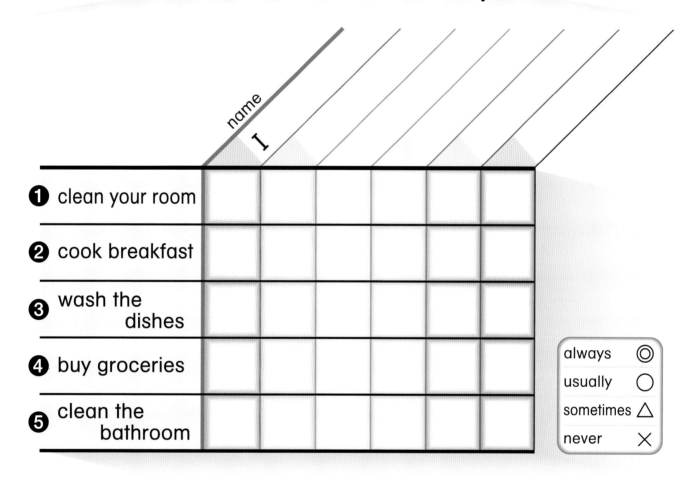

	name I					
❶ clean your room						
❷ cook breakfast						
❸ wash the dishes						
❹ buy groceries						
❺ clean the bathroom						

always	◎
usually	○
sometimes	△
never	✕

phonics

📢 **137**

ai			
	snail	train	nail

ie			
	tie	lie	pie

oa			
	boat	coat	soap

Stop playing the game. Stop playing the game.

You have to do your homework now.

Right now? Yes, right now!

Stop playing the game. Stop playing the game.

You have to take a bath now.

Right now? Yes, right now!

Stop playing the game. Stop playing the game.

You have to go to bed now.

Right now? Yes, right now!

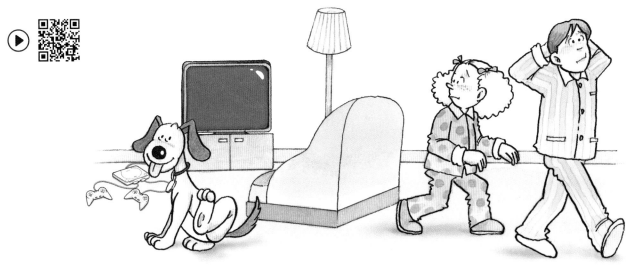

53

Words

stop talking · stop laughing · stop running · stop playing · stop writing · stop watching · stop walking

Communication activity

◉))165

- ○ Do you have to wash the dishes?
- ○ She has to wash the dishes.
- ○ She doesn't have to wash the dishes.

Do you have to ... tonight?

	do your homework	practice the piano	wash the dishes	go to *juku*
Jason	Yes, he does.	No, he doesn't.	Yes, he does.	No, he doesn't.
I				
friend				

I have to

I don't have to

has to

doesn't have to

What a pretty, what a pretty,

what a pretty girl I am!

What a noisy, what a noisy,

what a noisy girl you are!

What a rude, what a rude,

what a rude boy you are!

What a cool, what a cool,

what a cool boy I am!

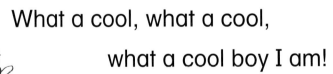

note

a big flower   What a big flower!

56

words

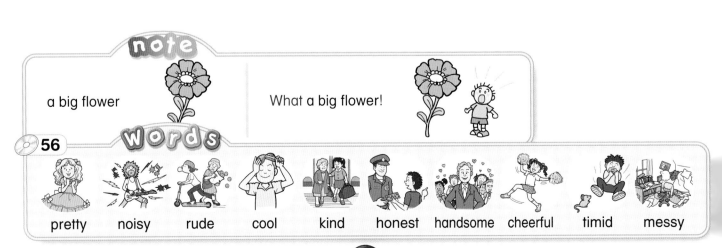

pretty   noisy   rude   cool   kind   honest   handsome   cheerful   timid   messy

Communication activity

◔ **What a cool boy I am!**

◔ **What a kind teacher I have!**

◀))**166**

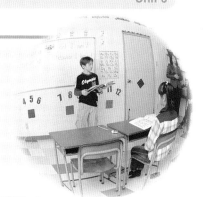

1

What a _____ (girl, boy) I am!

2

What a _____ (father, mother) I have!

3

What a _____ teacher I have!

4

What a _____ friend I have!

brave	strong	nice	tall	scary
smart	great	beautiful	young	your own idea

◀))**103**

1
- ⓐ Maki
- ⓑ Maki's mother
- ⓒ Maki's room

2
- ⓐ play baseball
- ⓑ No, she can't.
- ⓒ do her homework

3
- ⓐ studying
- ⓑ talking
- ⓒ shopping

4
- ⓐ right now
- ⓑ go to bed
- ⓒ ten o'clock

57→58

I am taller than Mary.

Jason is taller than me.

My mother is taller than Jason.

My father is taller than my mother.

My father is the tallest.

Mother is the strongest!

note

I am **tall**.

I am **taller**.

I am **the tallest**!

Words

59

tall → taller

long → longer

short → shorter

big → bigger

small → smaller

strong → stronger

good → better

bad → worse

Communication activity

- Who is taller, the mother or the father?
- The mother is taller than the father.
- The boy is the tallest.

◀)167

Which is bigger?

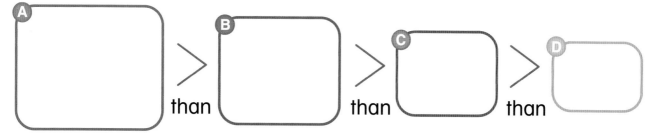

A > B than C than D than

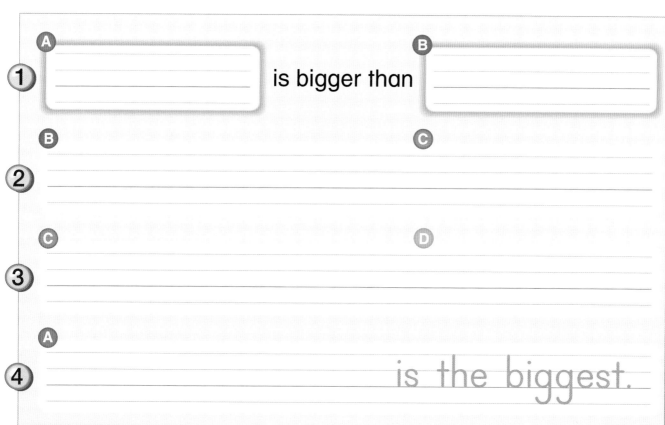

1. A _____ is bigger than B _____

2. B _____ C

3. C _____ D

4. A _____ is the biggest.

 Phonics

 ◀)138

 ph

photo   dolphin   elephant

 wh

what   whale   wheelchair

60 → 61

Where are you going?

To Hawaii.

When are you going?

On the ninth.

How are you going?

By airplane.

How long are you going to stay?

For five days.

Wow! You're a lucky boy. Have a good time.

Thank you.

62

Words

on Tuesday

on August 20th

in August

for one week

for two weeks

for three days

for one month

for one year

stay

lucky

1B

Communication activity

🔊168

- Where are you going?
- When are you going?
- How are you going?
- How long are you going to stay?

 Where are you going?

You To _____.

 When are you going?

You On _____.

 How are you going?

You By _____.

 How long are you going to stay?

You For _____.

 Have a good time.

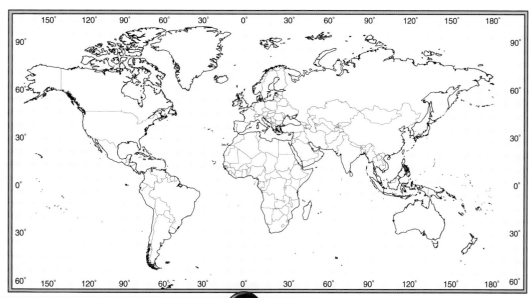

63→64

 I am ten years old.

I will be eleven years old tomorrow.

Tomorrow is my birthday.

I am ten years old, too.

I will be eleven years old next month.

Then you are younger than me!

Just by a month!

note

I am   ten years old now.

I will be eleven years old tomorrow.

65 Words

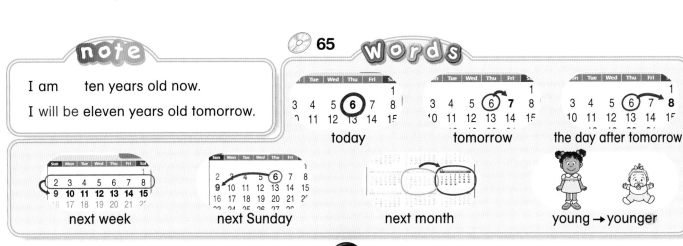

today

tomorrow

the day after tomorrow

next week

next Sunday

next month

young → younger

Communication activity

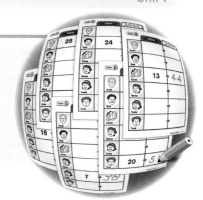

◀))169

○ In the year 2040, how old will you be?

○ I will be forty-four years old.

In the year 2040,

I will be

In the year _____,

1
- (a) by bus
- (b) to the library
- (c) by train

2
- (a) tomorrow
- (b) twelve years old
- (c) birthday party

3
- (a) The girl is.
- (b) I see a boy.
- (c) The girl can.

4
- (a) for two hours
- (b) two o'clock
- (c) homework

 Where do you want to go?

 I want to go to Japan.

I can speak Japanese. "Watashi no namae wa Tina desu."

 Where do you want to go?

 I want to go to France.

I can speak French. "Je m'appelle Shota."

I want to go to Spain.
I can speak Spanish. "Me llamo Sally."

I want to go to Italy.
I can speak Italian. "Mi chiamo Jim."

 note

I want a new bat.

I want to play baseball.

68

 Words

| Japan | France | Italy | Spain |
| Japanese | French | Italian | Spanish |

3B

Communication activity

◦)170

- ○ **Where do you want to go?**

- ○ **I want to go to France.**

① What do you want?

I want _____

② What do you want to do now?

I want to _____

I don't want to _____

③ Where do you want to go?

I want to go to _____

④ Do you want to speak English well?

Yes, _____ / No, _____

I _____

◦)139

ck

kick

chick

sick

ng

ring

song

king

69→70

I want something, something to eat.

A hot dog, French fries, pizza and pie.

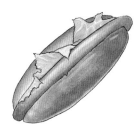   

I want something, something to drink.

Hot tea, iced tea, coffee and milk.

I want something, something to wear.

A heavy coat, a warm sweater, mittens and socks.

71

note

something to eat

something to drink

something to wear

words

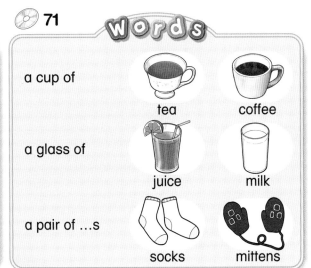

a cup of — tea — coffee

a glass of — juice — milk

a pair of ...s — socks — mittens

Communication activity

⦿ I want something to eat.

⦿ I have some cookies.

🔊171

1 I want something to eat.

_____

_____

_____

Anything else? _____

2 I want something to drink.

_____

_____

_____

Anything else? _____

3 I want something to wear.

_____

_____

_____

Anything else? _____

a hamburger	a sweater	a hot dog	tea
pants	a hat	a sandwich	milk
coffee	pizza	a coat	water

 72 → 73

We go to the bakery
　　　to buy some bread.

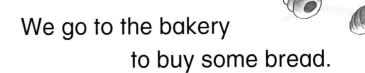

We go to the library
　　　to read some books.

We go to the park
　　　to ride a bike.

We go to school
　　　to do WHAT?

note

 I go to school　to study.

 I go to school　to meet friends.

74 **Words**

bakery

library

park

post office

restaurant

supermarket

hospital

bus stop

bank

city hall

department store

apartment building

Communication activity

 ◀))172

○ **We go to the post office to mail a letter.**

○ **We go to the post office to buy some stamps.**

① We go to the library ○	○	to eat dinner.
② We go to the restaurant ○	○	to read some books.
③ We go to the supermarket ○	○	to catch a bus.
④ We go to the bus stop ○	○	to mail a letter.
⑤ We go to the post office ○	○	to buy groceries.
⑥ We go to the park ○	○	to see a doctor.
⑦ We go to the hospital ○	○	to ride a bike.

I go to school to _____ .

study	eat lunch	meet friends	play in the playground
meet teachers	swim in the pool	play the piano	(your own idea)

1 How old is Anne?	
2 Where does she live?	
3 What does she like doing?	
4 What does she do in the park?	
5 Where does she go on the way home from the park?	
6 What does she buy?	

It was a strange dream!

In the dream I was a lion.

I was a big strong lion.

My name was Leo.

I was running in the jungle.

It was a strange dream!

In the dream I was a bird.

I was a big colorful bird.

I was a toucan.

I was flying over the jungle.

note

| I am a butterfly. | We are flying. |
| I was a caterpillar. | We were walking. |

77

Words

strange   dream   jungle   colorful   toucan   over

Communication activity

◉ What was the monkey doing?

◉ It was eating a banana under the chair.

It was a strange dream!

In the dream I was a _____

I was a _____

My name was _____

I was _____ ing _____

phonics

■))140

not	e

can pet pin hop cut

cane Pete pine hope cute

 Who took the cookies from the cookie jar?

 Jason took the cookies from the cookie jar.

 Who me?

 Yes, you!

 Not me!

 Then who?

 Daddy took the cookies from the cookie jar.

Oh, I did. They were very delicious.

cookie jar

80

Words

do your homework did your homework	take a cookie took a cookie	make a sandwich made a sandwich	go shopping went shopping	have a hot dog had a hot dog	read a book read a book

1B

Communication activity

- Who took the cookie from the cookie jar?
- Terry took the cookie from the cookie jar.

◄))174

◄))128

 You took the cookie!

 You Who me? Not me!

 What did you do yesterday?

You

 Where were you at eight o'clock last night?

You

 What were you doing at that time?

You

🎵 81   ***Do, did, did!***

① *Do did, Do did, Do did did,* Yeah, yeah, *Do did did!*

② *Take took, Take took, Take took took,* Yeah, yeah, *Take took took!*

③ *Make made, Make made, Make made made,* Yeah, yeah, *Make made made!*

④ *Go went, Go went, Go went went,* Yeah, yeah, *Go went went!*

⑤ *Have had, Have had, Have had had,* Yeah, yeah, *Have had had!*

⑥ *Read read, Read read, Read read read,* Yeah, yeah, *Read read read!*

⑦ *Cut cut, Cut cut, Cut cut cut,* Yeah, yeah, *Cut cut cut!*

82 → 83

Did you make your bed?

Yes, I did. Yes, I did.
I made my bed. Look!

Did you eat your lunch?

Yes, I did. Yes, I did.
I ate my lunch. Look!

Did you clean your room?

Yes, I did. Yes, I did.
I cleaned my room. Look!

Did you take a bath?

Yes, I did. Yes, I did.
I took a bath. Look!

84

Words

| make (my) bed | eat (my) lunch | clean (my) room | take a bath | study English | play soccer |
| made (my) bed | ate (my) lunch | cleaned (my) room | took a bath | studied English | played soccer |

Communication activity

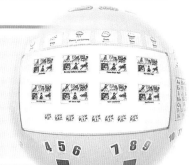

◉ On that day, I cleaned my room.

◉ I didn't do my homework.

◉ When was it?

🔊175

When was it?   It was

I

I

I

I

I

I

1
(a) I went to school.
(b) I left home at seven thirty.
(c) It was yesterday.

2
(a) Yes, I did.
(b) I went to the supermarket.
(c) It was in the morning.

3
(a) I have lunch.
(b) No, I didn't.
(c) I had some sandwiches.

4
(a) It was eight o'clock.
(b) I was at home.
(c) I was taking a bath.

Story: The Honest Woodcutter

Once upon a time, a woodcutter was cutting a branch off a tree in a forest.

"Oops!" His ax fell into a lake. He was sad.

A spirit appeared and said to him, "Why are you crying?"

"I lost my ax. It was an old ax but it was very important to me,"

the woodcutter answered.

The spirit went down into the water and came back with a golden ax.

"Is this yours?" the spirit asked. "No," the woodcutter answered.

"My ax is older than that one."

The spirit went down into the lake and came back with a silver ax.

"Is this yours?" the spirit asked. "No," the woodcutter answered.

"My ax is older than that one."

The spirit went down into the water again and came back with an iron ax.

"Is this yours?" the spirit asked. "Yes, that ax is mine!"

The woodcutter was very happy to see his old ax.

The spirit said, "You are an honest man.

I will give you all of them."

The woodcutter was very happy.

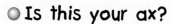

Communication activity

 ◀))176

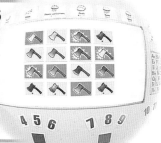

○ Is this your ax?

○ No, it isn't.
   The color is the same, but my ax is older than that one.

This is my friend _____ .

_____ is _____ than me.

I am _____ than _____ .

_____ is _____ than me.

I am _____ than _____ .

taller   shorter   stronger   older   younger

phonics

◀))141

 kn

knife

knee

knight

 gh

right

night

eight

Letter

Dear Friend,

Hello. My name is Tina. I'm eleven years old.

I'm in the fifth grade of Lakeside Elementary School.

My birthday is July 30th.

I live in Denver, Colorado, in the U.S.

Do you have a pet?

I have a dog. His name is Zippy.

I like to play tennis after school.

I can play the piano. Can you play the piano?

At school, I like math and music.

I don't like social studies.

Someday I want to go to Japan.

Please write me a letter.

Love, Tina

P.S. This is where I live.

○ **Who am I?**
○ **Please read sentence No.1.**
◀)177 ○ **You're Mr. Barton.**

Dear Friend,

Hello. My name is _____ . I'm _____ years old.

I'm in the _____ grade of _____ Elementary

School. My birthday is _____ .

I live in _____ .

I like to _____ after school.

I can _____ . Can you _____ ?

At school, I like _____ .

I don't like _____ .

Please write me a letter.

Love, _____

P.S. This is where I live.

◀)142

book

foot

wool

zoo

moon

root

This is my grandmother.

She is the principal of an elementary school.

She has two sons and one daughter.

She always gets up very early in the morning.

It takes her thirty minutes to go to her school by car.

She is cheerful and kind.

She works hard. Everyone likes her very much.

I am proud of my grandmother.

93

Words

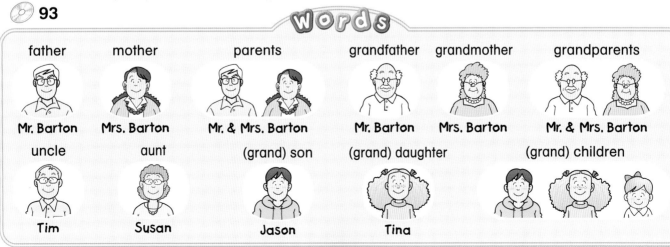

father	mother	parents	grandfather	grandmother	grandparents
Mr. Barton	Mrs. Barton	Mr. & Mrs. Barton	Mr. Barton	Mrs. Barton	Mr. & Mrs. Barton

uncle	aunt	(grand) son	(grand) daughter	(grand) children
Tim	Susan	Jason	Tina	

2B

Communication activity

🔊178

● I have a big brother and a little sister.

● I have an uncle and an aunt.

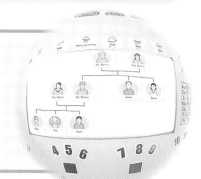

I am proud of my friend.

. Thank you.

1
- a) Yes, I did.
- b) Tom did.
- c) Susan did.

2
- a) to mail a letter
- b) to my uncle
- c) this afternoon

3
- a) Ken's mother.
- b) He lives in Paris.
- c) Ken's grandfather.

4
- a) at eight
- b) at six
- c) early

Story: It is important to learn a foreign language.

Once upon a time, a mother mouse lived with her baby mice in a small town.

She gave the baby mice lessons every day.

She said, "Bowwow, bowwow. Repeat after me!"

The baby mice repeated, "Bowwow, bowwow."

"Louder, please." The mother mouse said.

"Bowwow, bowwow." "Louder!"

"Bowwow, bowwow!" The baby mice practiced very hard.

The mother mouse and the baby mice had lessons day after day.

Repeat after me!

taking a walk

appeared

One day, when they were taking a walk in the town,

a big black cat appeared.

It tried to catch the baby mice and eat them!

The baby mice were very scared.

They could not even move.

very scared

But the mother mouse looked at the cat and shouted,

"Bowwow, bowwow!" in a big voice!

The baby mice followed their mother, saying,

"Bowwow, bowwow," in big voices.

surprised

BOW-WOW!

shouted

The cat was surprised and ran away. The cat thought that they were dogs.

The mother mouse turned around to the baby mice and said,

"Now you see why it is important to learn a foreign language."

ran away

Communication activity

🔊179

😊 Do you like dogs?
😊 Yes, I do.
😮 Yes, I do. I like dogs, too. Do you like dogs?
😊 No, I don't. I don't like dogs.

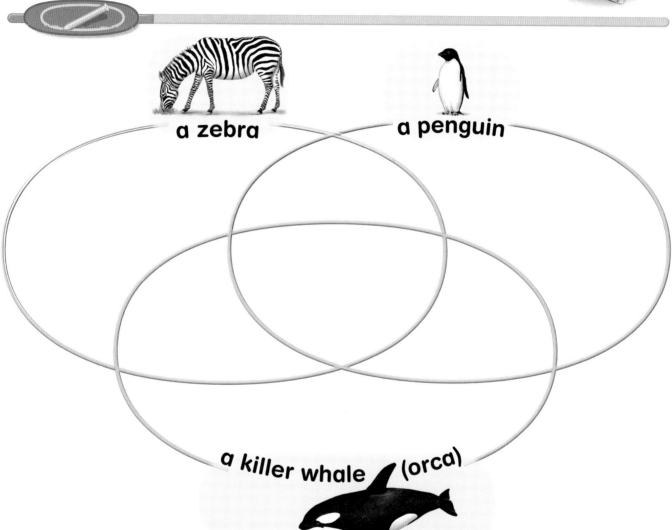

a zebra

a penguin

a killer whale (orca)

①	It has four legs.	⑥	It feeds its baby with milk.
②	It has two legs.	⑦	It can't fly.
③	It has no legs.	⑧	It can walk.
④	It is black and white.	⑨	It eats small fish.
⑤	It swims in the sea.	⑩	It lays eggs.

Song
Did You Ever See a Monster?

🔊 98

Did you ever see a monster,
a monster, a monster?

Did you ever see a monster
with red eyes and a tail?

Red eyes and a red tail,
a big nose and a big mouth.

Did you ever see a monster
with red eyes and a tail?

Song
A Tree in the Forest

By Catherine Steele

🔊 99

A tall tree stands in the forest.
A tall tree stands in the forest.
A tall tree stands in the forest.
On the other side of town.

On the tree there is a branch.
On the branch there is a twig.
On the twig there is a leaf.
Turning in the wind.

Yellow, red and brown.
Falling on the ground.
Yellow, red and brown.
Falling all around.

Song On Christmas Day

1. On Christmas Day hey hey hey hey,
We will have a tree hee hee hee hee,
And it will snow ho ho ho ho,
For you and me hee hee hee hee, (×2)

He wants a car. He wants a car.
And it will go brm brm brm brm,
brm brm brm brm. (×2)

2. On Christmas Day…

She wants a trumpet.
She wants a trumpet.
And it will go toot toot toot toot,
toot toot toot toot.
He wants a car. He wants a car.
And it will go brm brm brm brm,
brm brm brm brm.

On Christmas Day…

◀))100

Characters ◀)) 104

Tina Jason Mary Jim Sally Zippy Shota Mr. Kobayashi Mrs. Kobayashi Sakura

Unit 1 ① p.4 ◀)) 5

Words

sun tree moon sky mountain hill flower lake cloud star

...and more ◀)) 105

daffodil fireside rolling hills pond river sea rainbow earth

Unit 1 ② p.6 ◀)) 9

Words

in the ... grade first second third fourth fifth sixth

...and more ◀)) 106

Australia Brazil China Denmark Egypt France Germany Holland (the Netherlands) Italy

Japan Korea Laos Malaysia New Zealand Oman Portugal Qatar Russia

Spain Turkey United States of America Vietnam Sweden Mexico Yemen Zimbabwe

Unit 1 ③ p.8 ◀)) 12

My Family

Jim — my father

Sally — my mother

Jason — my big brother

Tina — me

Mary — my little sister

Zippy — my dog

...and more ◀)) 107

man woman car bike house play the piano play soccer play baseball

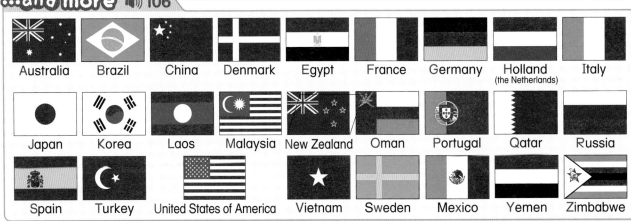
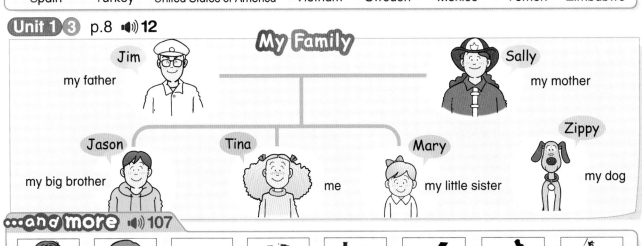

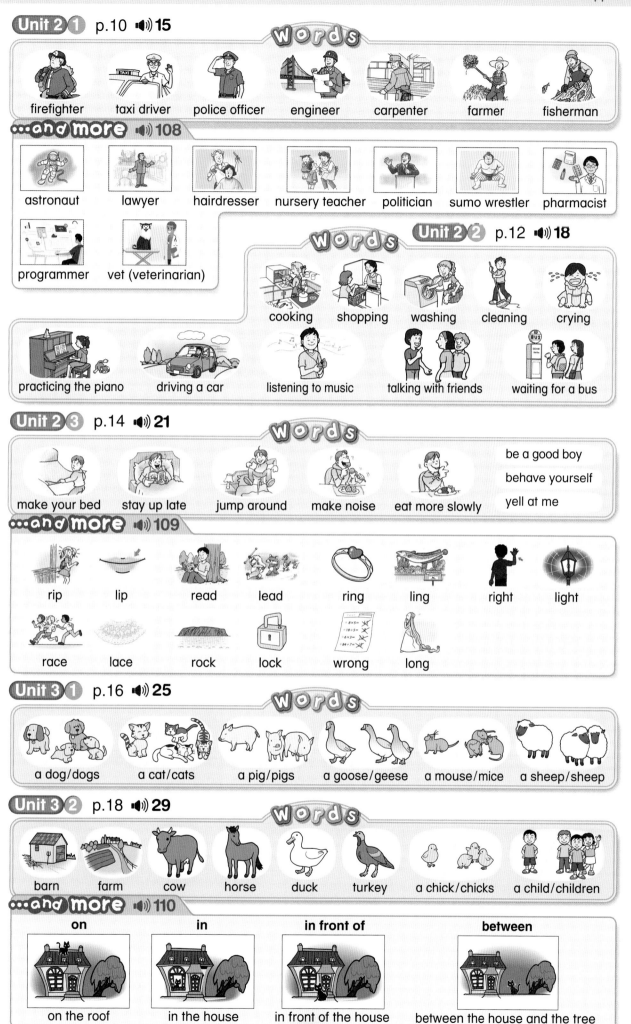

Unit 2 1 p.10 ◀)) **15**

words

firefighter · taxi driver · police officer · engineer · carpenter · farmer · fisherman

...and more ◀)) **108**

astronaut · lawyer · hairdresser · nursery teacher · politician · sumo wrestler · pharmacist

programmer · vet (veterinarian)

Unit 2 2 p.12 ◀)) **18**

words

cooking · shopping · washing · cleaning · crying

practicing the piano · driving a car · listening to music · talking with friends · waiting for a bus

Unit 2 3 p.14 ◀)) **21**

words

make your bed · stay up late · jump around · make noise · eat more slowly

be a good boy
behave yourself
yell at me

...and more ◀)) **109**

rip · lip · read · lead · ring · ling · right · light

race · lace · rock · lock · wrong · long

Unit 3 1 p.16 ◀)) **25**

words

a dog/dogs · a cat/cats · a pig/pigs · a goose/geese · a mouse/mice · a sheep/sheep

Unit 3 2 p.18 ◀)) **29**

words

barn · farm · cow · horse · duck · turkey · a chick/chicks · a child/children

...and more ◀)) **110**

on · **in** · **in front of** · **between**

on the roof · in the house · in front of the house · between the house and the tree

Unit 4 1 p.22 🔊 35

Words

dive

win

score a goal

score a basket

jump over

I made it!

You made it!

bake a cake

ride a unicycle

make a speech

Unit 4 2 p.24 🔊 39

Words

wheelchair

athlete

smart

guide dog

great

I'm proud of …

everywhere

Unit 4 3 p.26 🔊 42

Words

very well

How are you?
I am glad to meet you.
I'm …

Hi!

I can speak English very well.

a little

How are you?
I... I...
I am …

I can speak English a little.

not ... at all

I cannot speak English at all.

...and more 🔊 111

swim

play the piano

play the recorder

ski

cook

speak French

speak English

write English

Unit 5 1 p.28 🔊 45

Words

live→lives

have→has

like→likes

go→goes

speak→speaks

eat→eats

mean→means

🔊 112

best friend

cherry blossoms

bridge
build a bridge

college
go to college

...and more 🔊 113-114

ant

bee

penguin

kangaroo

panda

zebra

bear

killer whale (orca)

honey

sugar

bamboo

grass

a pocket

fins

wings

Unit 5 3 p.32 🔊 50

Words

clean (your) room

cook breakfast

wash the dishes

buy groceries

clean the bathroom

feed the pet

...and more 🔊 115

$\frac{100}{100}$ いつも！かならず
always

約80
$\frac{80}{100}$ ふつうは いつもは
usually

約50
$\frac{50}{100}$ ときどき
sometimes

$\frac{0}{100}$ 1度もない ぜったい〜ない
never

Unit 6 ① p.34 ◀))53

Words

stop talking	stop laughing	stop running	stop playing	stop writing	stop watching	stop walking

…and more ◀))116

do your homework	practice the piano	wash the dishes	go to *juku*

Unit 6 ② p.36 ◀))56

Words

pretty	noisy	rude	cool	kind	honest	handsome	cheerful	timid	messy

Unit 6 ③ p.38 ◀))59

Words

tall → taller   long → longer   short → shorter   big → bigger

small → smaller   strong → stronger   good → better   bad → worse

…and more ◀))117

tall → taller   short → shorter   big → bigger   strong → stronger

the tallest   the shortest   the biggest   the strongest

long → longer   small → smaller   good → better   bad → worse

the longest   the smallest   the best   the worst

Unit 7 ① p.40 ◀))62

Words

on Tuesday	on August 20th	in August	for one week	for two weeks

for three days	for one month	for one year	stay	lucky

…and more ◀))118

Hawaii	Paris	London	Sydney	Kyoto	New York	car

airplane	train	ship	ferry	truck	bike	motorbike

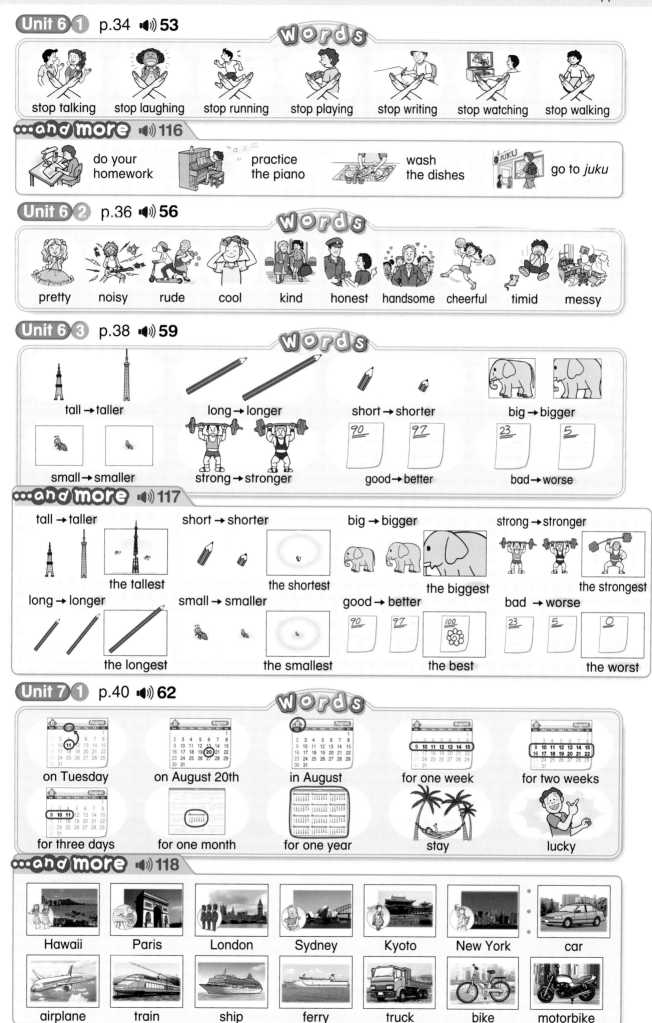

Unit 7 ② p.42 🔊 119

Words

 today

 tomorrow

 the day after tomorrow

  2040年 the year 2040 twenty forty / the year twenty forty

 next week

tomorrow next Sunday

next month

 young → younger

Unit 7 ③ p.44 🔊 120

Words

 こんにちは Japan → Japanese

 Bonjour. France → French

Ciao. Italy → Italian

Hola. Spain → Spanish

Unit 8 ① p.46 🔊 121·122·123

to eat

 some spaghetti   some pizza   some bread   some cookies   some candy   some chocolate

to drink

a cup of tea   a cup of coffee   a glass of juice   a glass of milk   a glass of water   a cup of hot chocolate

to wear

a pair of socks   a pair of mittens   a pair of pants   a pair of glasses   a pair of slippers   a pair of gloves

Unit 8 ② p.48 🔊 74

Words

bakery   library   park   post office   restaurant   supermarket

hospital   bus stop   bank   city hall   department store   apartment building

...and more 🔊 124

to read some books   to study   to borrow books   to ride a bike   to walk our dog   to have a picnic   to mail a letter

to buy some stamps   to deposit money   to have breakfast   to have lunch   to have dinner   to buy some bread   to buy groceries

to buy toilet paper   to see a doctor   to have a health check   to get a prescription   to catch a bus   to meet a friend   to check the timetable

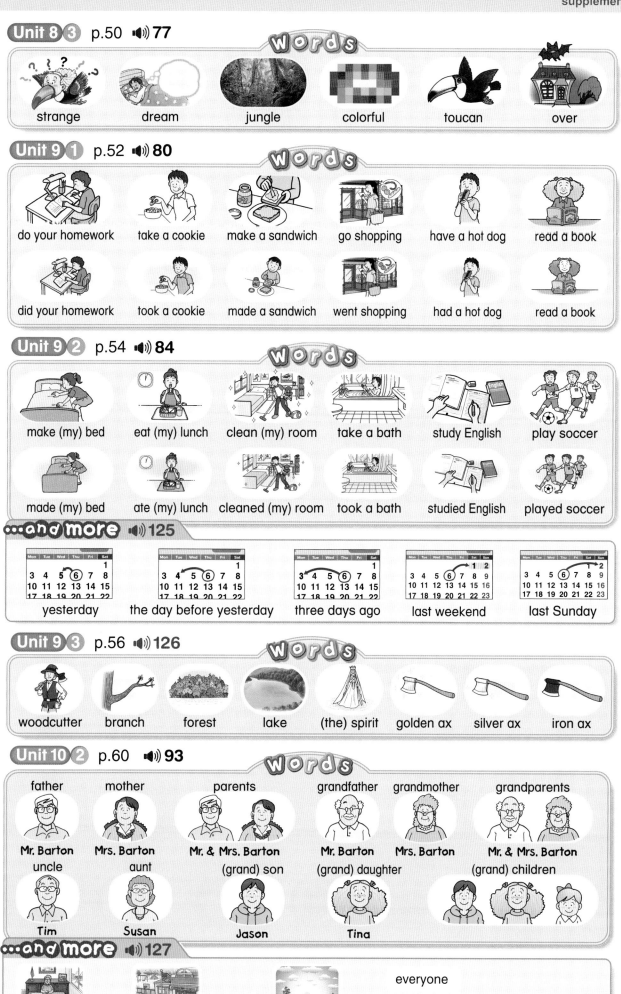

Unit 8 3 p.50 🔊 **77**

Words

strange | dream | jungle | colorful | toucan | over

Unit 9 1 p.52 🔊 **80**

Words

do your homework | take a cookie | make a sandwich | go shopping | have a hot dog | read a book

did your homework | took a cookie | made a sandwich | went shopping | had a hot dog | read a book

Unit 9 2 p.54 🔊 **84**

Words

make (my) bed | eat (my) lunch | clean (my) room | take a bath | study English | play soccer

made (my) bed | ate (my) lunch | cleaned (my) room | took a bath | studied English | played soccer

…and more 🔊 125

yesterday | the day before yesterday | three days ago | last weekend | last Sunday

Unit 9 3 p.56 🔊 **126**

Words

woodcutter | branch | forest | lake | (the) spirit | golden ax | silver ax | iron ax

Unit 10 2 p.60 🔊 **93**

Words

father | mother | parents | grandfather | grandmother | grandparents

Mr. Barton | Mrs. Barton | Mr. & Mrs. Barton | Mr. Barton | Mrs. Barton | Mr. & Mrs. Barton

uncle | aunt | (grand) son | (grand) daughter | | (grand) children

Tim | Susan | Jason | Tina

…and more 🔊 127

principal | elementary school | early in the morning

everyone

It takes her … minutes to …

supplement

◀))129

Where is the bus stop?

Walk, walk, walk. Walk along the street.

Turn right at the second corner, and walk two more blocks.

You'll find the bus stop on your left.

You cannot miss it! It's on your left.

I'm here.

Go straight.	Turn left.	Turn right.	Cross the street.	next to …	across from …

Signs

◀))130

 Staff Only
 Closed
 Hands Off
 One Way
 Keep Off the Grass
 Fire Exit

 Do Not Cross
 Dead End
 Pull
 Wait Here
 Keep Left
 Out of Order

→Workbook p.10

🔊131

You How do you say "kantan" in English?

friend Easy.

You How do you spell it?

friend E-a-s-y, easy.

You That's easy!

You Then how do you say "muzukashii" in English?

friend Difficult.

You Excuse me?

friend Difficult.

You How do you spell it?

friend D-i-f-f-i-c-u-l-t, difficult.

You That IS difficult!!!

My Own Dictionary

覚えておきたい単語や表現、英文を書きとめておこう！

1. How many days are there in a week?

days

2. How many hours are there in a day?

hours

3. How many days are there in a year?

days

4. How many minutes are there in one hour?

minutes

5. How many seconds are there in one minute?

seconds

6. How many seconds are there in one hour?

seconds

7. How high is Mt. Fuji?

meters

Let's read numbers!

◀)) 132

1	one
10	ten
100	one hundred
1,000	one thousand
10,000	ten thousand
100,000	one hundred thousand
1,000,000	one million
10,000,000	ten million
100,000,000	one hundred million
1,000,000,000	one billion
10,000,000,000	ten billion

phonics

ch sh th ： ph wh ： ck ng 2つ並ぶと、まったく新しい音になります。

 ◀))133

| ch |  church | rich | sh | sheep | ship | th | math | father | mother |

ph photo　 dolphin　 elephant

wh what　 whale　 wheelchair

ck kick　 chick　 sick

ng ring　 song　 king

ee ea ： ai ie oa 2つ並んだ時、前の文字をアルファベットの名前で読みます。（2つめの文字は読みません）

ee see　 bee　 meet

ea sea　 tea　 meat

ai snail　 train　 nail

ie tie　 lie　 pie

oa boat　 coat　 soap

e ことばの最後に読まないeがくる時、その前の母音は
アルファベットの名前で読みます。

e　 can　 pet　 pin　 hop　 cut

 ◀))134　 cane　 Pete　 pine　 hope　 cute

kn gh k(n)で始まる時、ことばの真ん中に
ghがくる時、kとghは読みません。

kn knife　knee　knight

gh right　night　eight

c g cとgの後にe , i , yがくる時、発音が変わります。

c city　 cent　 cat

g giant　 gym　 gun

oo oが2つ並ぶ時、新しい音になります。
ooには短い音と長い音があります。

oo book　 foot　 wool

oo zoo　moon　root

bl cr dr fr sk spr str 2つまたは3つの連続する子音をすばやく読みます。

| blue | crab | dress | frog | skip | spring | street |

supplement phonics Let's read aloud.

ch sh th : ph wh : ck ng   c   g   ee ea : ai ie oa

A

B

C

R

1. I know his name. (   )

2. Wash your hands with soap. (   )

3. Look at the big elephant in the zoo. (   )

4. You can paint your desk green. (   )

5. I like to fish in a lake. (   )

6. This book is mine. (   )

Q

7. I am a good teacher. (   )

8. Pete can stand on one foot. (   )

9. A fat frog is at the top of a tree. (   )

N

P

O

M

e : kn gh oo fr gr pl st tr str

D E F

G

10 I like to read books. (   )

11 Please stand in front of my desk. (   )

12 I read three books at night. (   )

13 My mother is not strict. (   )

14 I hope to take a trip to the moon. (   )

15 Did you see me help the old man? (   )

16 Pete and I run to the church on Sunday.
(   )

17 I know the sick man in the bed. (   )

18 The king and queen ate a big sandwich
for lunch in the city. (   )

H

I

L

K

J

Learning World ③ Syllabus

Unit	Topics	Grammar	Structures	Words and Phrases レッスンで使うおもな語彙 (太字はwordsコーナーの語彙)	Phonics/Listening Test/Song
1-1	私の好きなもの I love our Earth.	•復習		**sun, tree, moon, sky, mountain, hill, flower, lake, cloud, star** daffodil, fireside, rolling hills / pond, river, sea, rainbow, earth	♪ I Love the Mountains
1-2	私たちの町 We love our city.	•復習		**in the ... grade / first, second, third, fourth, fifth, sixth** Australia, Brazil, China, Denmark, Egypt, France, Germany, Holland (the Netherlands), Italy, Japan, Korea, Laos, Malaysia, New Zealand, Oman, Portugal, Qatar, Russia, Spain, Turkey, United States of America, Vietnam, Sweden, Mexico, Yemen, Zimbabwe	Listening Test
1-3	Tinaの家族 Tina's family	•復習		**My Family: my father, my mother, my big brother, me, my little sister, my dog** man, woman / car, bike, house / play the piano, play soccer, play baseball	Survival English
2-1	お母さんは消防士 Mother is a fire fighter.	•職業の聞き方、答え方	■What does he do? ■He is a taxi driver.	**firefighter, taxi driver, police officer, engineer, carpenter, farmer, fisherman** astronaut, lawyer, hairdresser, nursery teacher, politician, sumo wrestler, pharmacist, programmer, vet (veterinarian)	
2-2	いそがしい一日 A busy day	•現在進行形 (復習)	■I am running.	**cooking, shopping, washing, cleaning, crying, practicing the piano, driving a car, listening to music, talking with friends, waiting for a bus**	Listening Test
2-3	こわいお母さん① My scary mother 1	•命令形 / 否定命令形	■Go out. ■Don't go out.	**make your bed, stay up late, jump around, make noise, eat more slowly,** be a good boy, behave yourself, yell at me	♪ Did you ever see a lassie? Listening Activity: r / l
3-1	A dog or dogs?	•名詞の単数形 複数形	■How many geese? Five geese.	**a dog-dogs, a cat-cats, a pig-pigs, a goose-geese, a mouse-mice, a sheep-sheep**	♪ One Man Went to Mow
3-2	あら、まあ 大変 Oh, my God!	•There is ... There are ...	■There is a cow on the pig. ■There are chicks on the turkey.	**barn, farm, cow, horse, duck, turkey, a chick-chicks, a child-children** on the roof, in the house, in front of the house, **between** the house and the tree	♪ Old MacDonald Had a Farm Listening Test
3-3	駐車場で At a parking lot	•形容詞	■Three beautiful small shiny new yellow cars.		Phonics (c, g)
4-1	君ならできる! You can do it!	•助動詞 can (復習)	■I can't swim. ■Yes, you can.	**dive, win, score a goal, score a basket, jump over, bake a cake, ride a unicycle, make a speech,** I made it! You made it!	♪ What Can You Do?
4-2	ぼくの誇り I'm proud of my friend.	•助動詞 can (復習) •be proud of ...	■I am proud of my friend. ■He can go everywhere.	**wheelchair, athlete, smart, guide dog, great,** I'm proud of..., everywhere	Listening Test
4-3	日本語が話せますか? Can you speak Japanese?	•程度を表す副詞	■I can speak English very well. ■I can't speak French at all.	**very well, a little, not ... at all** swim, play the piano, play the recorder, ski, cook, speak French, speak English, write English	Phonics (ee, ea)
5-1	翔太と、翔太の家族 Shota and his family	•動詞の三人称単数現在 (肯定文、否定文)	■I have... You have... ■He has... She has...	**live-lives, have-has, like-likes, go-goes, speak-speaks, eat-eats,** mean-means / best friend, cherry blossoms, build a bridge, go to college ant, bee, penguin, kangaroo, panda, zebra, bear, killer whale (orca) honey, sugar, bamboo, grass, a pocket, fins, wings	
5-2	私は人気者 Everyone likes me.	•動詞の三人称単数現在 (疑問文)	■Does she like me? Yes, she does. / No, she doesn't.		Listening Test
5-3	家事の役割分担 House chores	•疑問詞whoで始まる文	■Who cleans your room? ■I do. ■My father does.	**clean (your) room, cook breakfast, wash the dishes, buy groceries, clean the bathroom, feed the pet** always, usually, sometimes, never	Phonics (ai, ie, oa)
6-1	こわいお母さん② My scary mother 2	•have to ... •stop ...ing	■Stop playing the game. ■You have to go to bed.	**stop talking, stop laughing, stop running, stop playing, stop writing, stop watching, stop walking** do your homework, practice the piano, wash the dishes, go to juku	

Unit	Title	Grammar	Example sentences	Vocabulary	Phonics / Listening
6-2	なんて私は可愛いのでしょう！ What a pretty girl I am!	●感嘆文	■What a big flower!	**pretty, noisy, rude, cool, kind, honest, handsome, cheerful, timid, messy**	Listening Test
6-3	背くらべ Who is taller?	●比較級 / 最上級	■I am tall. ■I am taller. ■I am the tallest.	**tall- taller, long- longer, short- shorter, big- bigger, small-smaller, strong- stronger, good-better, bad-worse** / the tallest, the shortest, the biggest, the strongest, the longest, the smallest, the best, the worst	Phonics (ph, wh)
7-1	楽しんできてね Have a good time!	●近未来を表す進行形 ●wh で始まる疑問詞 (復習)	■Where are you going? ■I'm going to Hawaii.	**on Tuesday, on August 20th, in August, for two weeks, for three days, for one year, stay, lucky** / Hawaii, Paris, London, Sydney, Kyoto, New York/ car, airplane, train, ship, ferry, truck, bike, motorbike	
7-2	Tina はもうすぐ11歳 Tina will be eleven years old.	●未来形 will (be)	■I will be eleven years old tomorrow.	**today, tomorrow, the day after tomorrow, next week, next Sunday, next month, young-younger** the year 2040	Listening Test
7-3	行ってみたい国 I want to go to...	●不定詞 名詞用法	■I want to play baseball.	**Japan – Japanese** – Konnichiwa. **France – French** – Bonjour. **Italy – Italian** – Ciao. **Spain – Spanish** – Hola.	Phonics (ck, ng)
8-1	何か食べ物をください Please give me something to eat.	●不定詞 形容詞用法 ●a cup of … ●a glass of … ●a pair of …s	■I want something to eat. I want something to drink. I want something to wear.	**a cup of tea, a cup of coffee, a glass of juice, a glass of milk** / a glass of water, a cup of hot chocolate **a pair of socks, a pair of mittens** / a pair of pants, a pair of glasses, a pair of slippers, a pair of gloves / some spaghetti, some pizza, some bread, some cookies, some candy, some chocolate	
8-2	学校に、何をするために行くの？ Why do you go to school?	●不定詞 副詞用法	■I go to school to study. I go to school to meet friends.	**bakery, library, park, post office, restaurant, supermarket, hospital, bus stop, bank, city hall, department store, apartment building** to read some books, to study, to borrow books / to ride a bike, to walk our dog, to have a picnic / to mail a letter, to buy some stamps, to deposit money / to have breakfast, to have lunch, to have dinner / to buy some bread, to buy groceries, to buy toilet paper/to see a doctor, to have a health check, to get a prescription / to catch a bus, to meet a friend, to check the timetable	Listening Test
8-3	不思議な夢 A strange dream	●be動詞の過去形 ●過去進行形	■I am a butterfly. I was a caterpillar. ■We are flying. We were walking.	**strange, dream, jungle, colorful, toucan, over**	Phonics (silent e)
9-1	だれがクッキーを取ったの？ Who took the cookie?	●動詞の過去形 (肯定文) ●疑問詞who で始まる文 (復習)	■Who took the cookie? ■Jason took the cookie.	**do-did your homework, take-took a cookie, make-made a sandwich, go-went shopping, have-had a hot dog, read-read a book**	🔊 Do, did, did
9-2	ちゃんとやったでしょう！ Look! I did!	●動詞の過去形 (疑問文、否定文)	■I made my bed. ■I didn't make my bed. ■Did you make your bed?	**make-made (my) bed, eat-ate (my) lunch, clean-cleaned (my) room, take-took a bath, study-studied English, play-played soccer** yesterday, the day before yesterday, three days ago, last weekend, last Sunday	Listening Test
9-3	Story 1: 金の斧 銀の斧 The Honest Woodcutter	●Story (比較級の復習)	■My ax is older than that one. The color is the same.	woodcutter, branch, forest, lake, (the) spirit, golden ax, silver ax, iron ax	Phonics (kn, gh)
10-1	Tinaからの手紙 A letter from Tina	●Letter (総復習)		Tina, Jason, Mr. Barton, Mrs. Barton, Shota, Mr. Kobayashi, Mrs. Kobayashi	Phonics (oo)
10-2	おばあちゃんが大好き I love my grandmother.	●Speech (総復習)		**father, mother, parents, grandmother, grandfather, grandparents, uncle, aunt, (grand) son, (grand) daughter, (grand) children** / Tina Barton, Jason Barton, Mary Barton, Jim Barton, Sally Barton, Tim, Susan, Mr. Barton, Mrs. Barton, principal, elementary school, early in the morning / everyone, It takes her …minutes to …	Listening Test
10-3	Story 2: 外国語を勉強することは大切です It is important to learn a foreign language.	●Story (総復習)			

notes

Unit 2 2 p.12
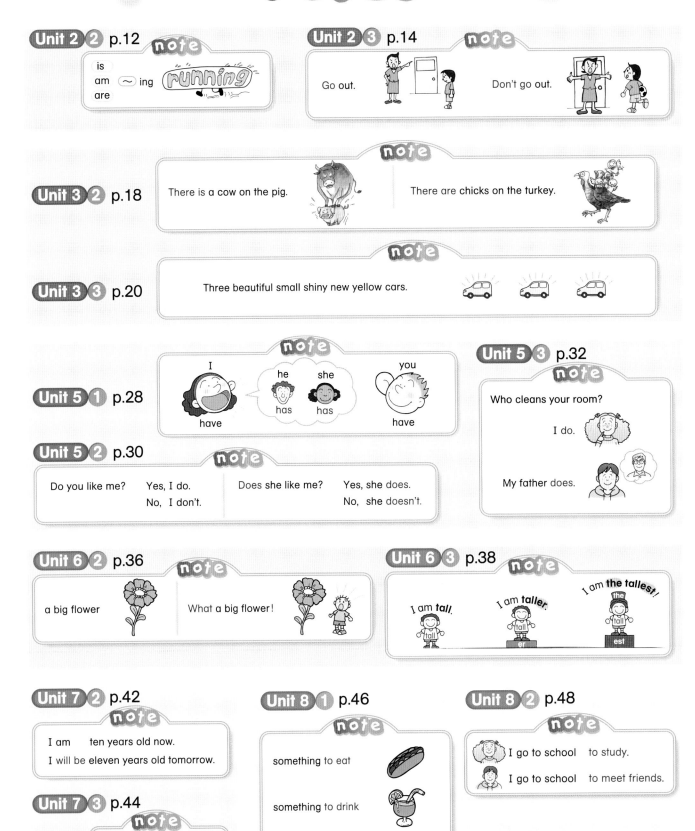

is
am ～ ing **running**
are

Unit 2 3 p.14

Go out.

Don't go out.

Unit 3 2 p.18

There is a cow on the pig.

There are chicks on the turkey.

Unit 3 3 p.20

Three beautiful small shiny new yellow cars.

Unit 5 1 p.28

I
he she
has has
you
have have

Unit 5 3 p.32

Who cleans your room?

I do.

My father does.

Unit 5 2 p.30

Do you like me?   Yes, I do.
              No, I don't.

Does she like me?   Yes, she does.
              No, she doesn't.

Unit 6 2 p.36

a big flower

What a big flower!

Unit 6 3 p.38

I am **tall**.

I am **taller**.

I am **the tallest!**

Unit 7 2 p.42

I am   ten years old now.
I will be eleven years old tomorrow.

Unit 8 1 p.46

something to eat

something to drink

something to wear

Unit 8 2 p.48

I go to school   to study.

I go to school   to meet friends.

Unit 7 3 p.44

I want a new bat.

I want to play baseball.

Unit 8 3 p.50

I am   a butterfly.
I was a caterpillar.

We are   flying.
We were walking.

My name is

_____

PROGRESS REPORT

4	24	44
6	26	46
8	28	48
10	30	50
12	32	52
14	34	54
16	36	56
18	38	58
20	40	60
22	42	62

Challenge Chart

Date	1	2	3	4	5	6	7	8	9	10	11	12	Total

Date	1	2	3	4	5	6	7	8	9	10	11	12	Total

先生の質問に答えて色をぬりましょう。

Students color in one happy face at a time on answering each of the teacher's questions during warm up/review time.

Certificate of Achievement

Learning World 3

Awarded to _____

this _____ day of _____,

for your great effort in

Learning World BOOK 3

Signed